# BIG GOD
## Little Me
# ACTIVITY BOOK

*Big God, Little Me Activity Book*

Published in 2019 by Kregel Children's Books, an imprint of Kregel Inc.,

2450 Oak Industrial Dr. NE, Grand Rapids, MI 49505 USA

Previously published in 2018 under the title *Children's Activity Bible*



Drejervej 15 3rd floor, DK 2400 Copenhagen NV, Denmark

Email: info@sph.as

www.sph.as



Activities and layout by Isabelle Gao

Graphic design by Gao Hanyu

ISBN 978-0-8254-4642-9

Printed in China

# BIG GOD
## Little Me
# ACTIVITY BOOK

Stories retold by Leyah Jensen and Isabelle Gao
Illustrated by José Pérez Montero

KREGEL
CHILDREN'S BOOKS

# Contents

## THE NEW TESTAMENT

* Asterisks mark stories that do not appear in *Big God, Little Me: An Ask and Learn Storybook Bible*. Bonus content provides additional activities and learning about God and His Word.

# THE OLD TESTAMENT

# God Makes the World

Genesis 1:1–19

In the beginning, there was nothing but darkness.

There was no water and no land, no animals and no people. But in the silence, there was God. God had a plan. "Let there be light!" He said.

God divided the light from the darkness. He called the light *day*, and the darkness *night*.

Then God stretched out space deep and wide. He placed the planets and the stars in the sky right where He wanted them.

# FIND THE DIFFERENT EARTH

Circle the earth that is different from the other ones.

1

2

3

4

# WORD SEARCH

Find the words hidden in the grid.

EARTH

DARK

| | | | | | |
|---|---|---|---|---|---|
| A | E | X | I | L | S |
| D | A | R | K | T | U |
| P | R | M | O | O | N |
| S | T | A | R | G | W |
| Q | H | B | J | U | C |
| L | I | G | H | T | F |

STAR

MOON

LIGHT

SUN

# God Fills the Earth

Genesis 1:20–25

God created water and land, and He made plants grow.

He filled the oceans with fish of amazing shapes and colors.

God made birds to fly. Then He made animals of every kind to live on land. Some creatures were large and some were small. Some were spiky and some were soft.

God created all of them, big and small, and He liked everything He made.

# SPOT THE DIFFERENCES

Can you find the 7 differences between these 2 pictures?

# ADD UP

Add up the penguins and write down the number for each line.

 +  =

 +  =

 +  =

 +  =

# Adam and Eve

Genesis 1:26–3:24

God had one last creation—people!

God made a man and named him Adam. Then He made a woman and named her Eve. Adam and Eve loved each other very much.

God told Adam and Eve to take good care of the animals. Then

they all lived together peacefully in a beautiful garden in a place called Eden. They could eat any fruit they wanted . . . except the fruit from one tree. But one day, an evil snake tricked them into eating it anyway.

When God learned that they had disobeyed, He was very, very sad. He sent them away from the garden to never come back.

# COMPLETE THE PICTURE

Find out where the missing pieces belong and draw a line to their correct places.

1

2

3

4

5

# DOT-TO-DOT

Connect the dots to see which fruit Adam and Eve ate from the tree. Then color it.

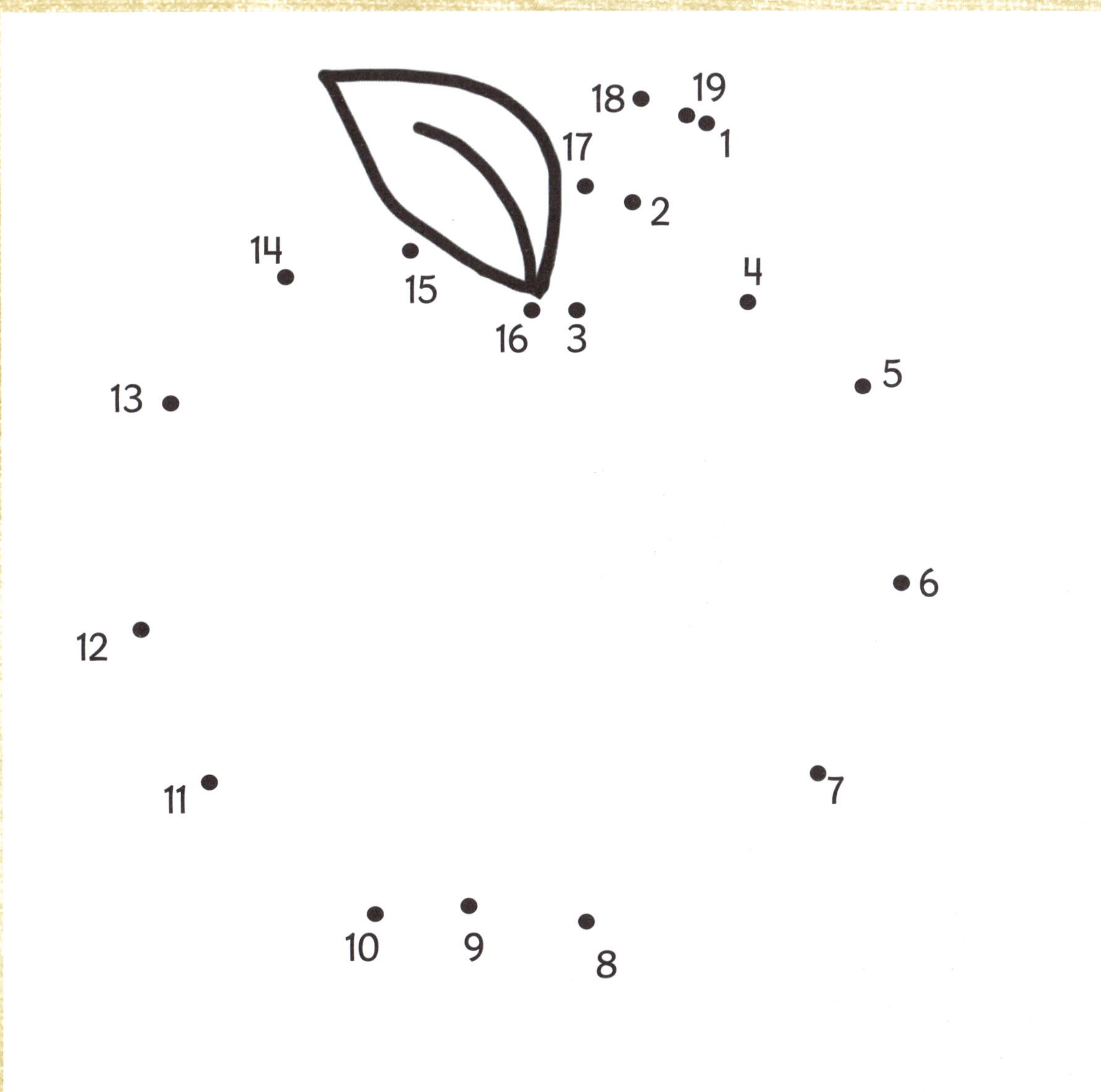

# Cain and Abel

Genesis 4:1–18

Adam and Eve made a home for themselves outside of the garden. Soon Eve gave birth to a baby and named him Cain. Then they had another baby boy and named him Abel.

Cain and Abel each had a special job. Abel took care of the animals, while Cain took care of the fields. Cain gave God some of the food from his harvest. But Abel gave God his best lamb. When God saw the gifts, He was happier that Abel gave his best. This made Cain very jealous of his brother.

Cain told Abel to come out into the field with him. Then Cain attacked his brother and killed him! God was so angry that He sent Cain away from home, telling him that he would never be able to grow anything again.

# FIND THE PAIR

Find the 2 pictures of Abel that are exactly the same.

# MATCH THE PARTS

Draw a line to match the 2 parts of the same animal.

# Noah and the Ark

Genesis 6:5–22

Noah was a good man. He loved God. But the rest of the world had stopped listening to God. People were violent and sinful. So God told Noah, "I'm going to send a flood to destroy the world, but I have a job for you."

God told Noah to build a special boat called an ark. "Make it big," God said. The boat needed to have many floors with many rooms and a big door in the side. After months of hard work, the boat was finished. God told Noah, "Bring a male and a female of each kind of animal."

Two by two, the animals were led into the boat by Noah.

# COLOR THE ANIMALS

Use your colored pencils to complete the picture.

# FIND THE ARK

Help the ostriches find the boat.

# The Great Flood

Genesis 7:13–8:19

Noah and his family went into the boat with all the animals and closed the door. Then the rain began to fall. Soon the whole world was flooded with water. Noah's boat floated safely on top of the waves.

After forty days and nights, the rain finally stopped.

Noah sent out a dove in search of land. The dove flew back to the boat with an olive branch in its beak!

God told Noah, "The flood is over." So Noah opened the great big door, and all the animals came out onto dry land.

# FIND THE DIFFERENT DOVE

Which dove is different from the other ones?

1

2

3

4

# DIFFERENT SIZES

Which bird is the biggest? Which is the smallest?

# Noah and God's Gift

Genesis 8:20–9:16

Noah and his family were grateful that God had saved them from the flood. Everyone praised God. Noah built an altar where he gave God gifts to thank Him for keeping them safe.

Then God made three promises to Noah. The first promise was that there would always be seasons . . . summer, fall, winter, and spring.

God also said that there would always be night and day. His last promise was that He would never again flood the whole earth. To make sure that people never forgot this promise, He left a special reminder.

God placed a beautiful rainbow
in the sky for everyone to see!

# COLOR BY NUMBERS

Color the rainbow by following the numbers.

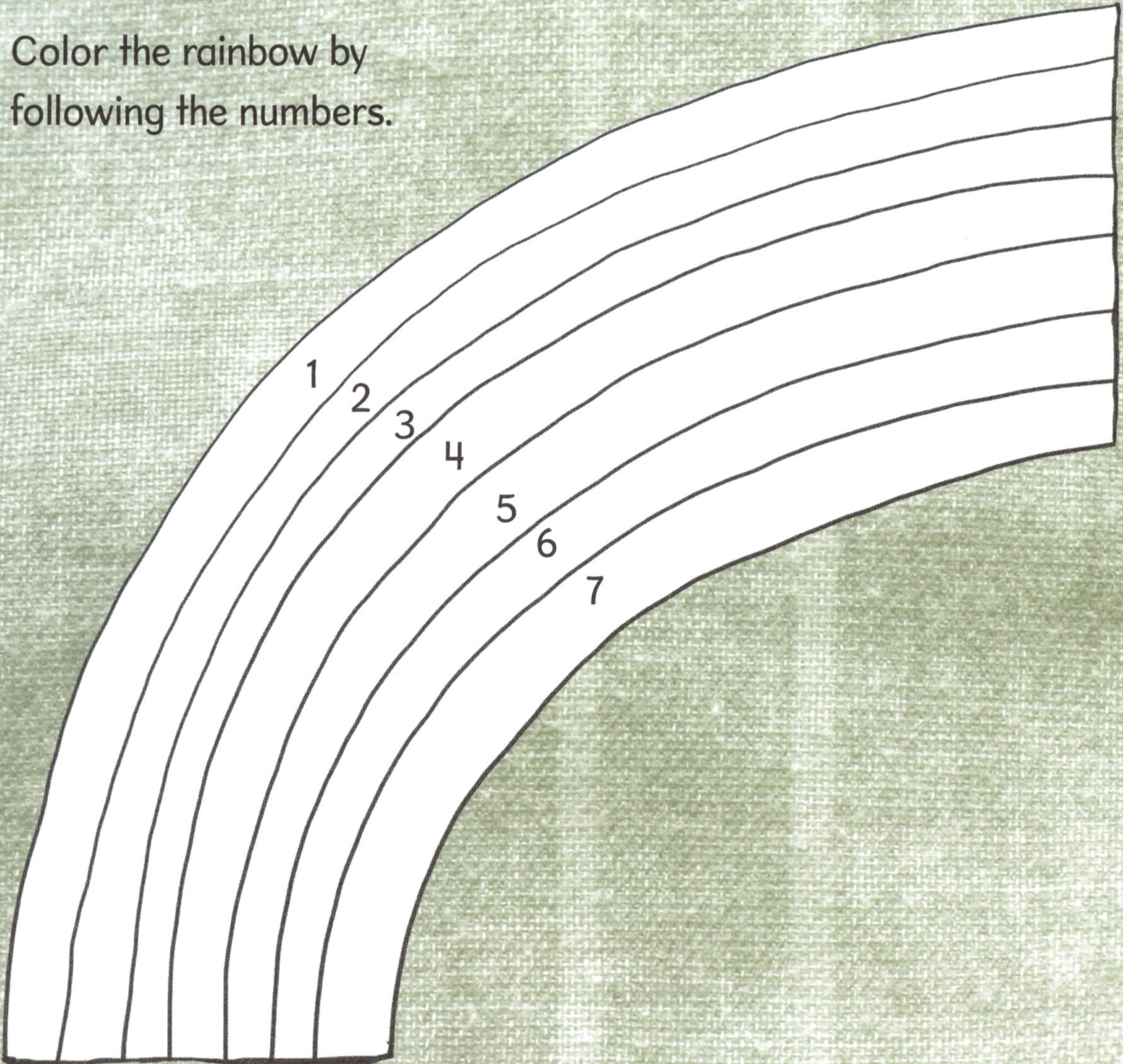


1 Red

2 Orange

3 Yellow

4 Green

5 Blue

6 Purple

7 Violet

# WRITE THE COLORS

Trace over the names of the colors.

RED
ORANGE
YELLOW
GREEN
BLUE
PURPLE
VIOLET

# The Tower of Babel

Genesis 10:32–11:9

Soon the world was filled with people again. Some of them settled in a place called Babel. The people in Babel decided to build a tower so high that it would reach heaven. "We will be famous, and God will be pleased with us!" they said to one another.

But when God saw the tall tower, He was not pleased. He saw that the people of Babel were no longer humble servants.

Instead, they were proud—believing they could reach God with their high tower. He punished the people by giving them each their own language.

# SPOT THE DIFFERENCES

Can you find the 7 differences between these 2 pictures?

# FIND THE PAIR

Find the 2 pictures that are exactly the same.

# Abraham Follows God

Genesis 12–13, 17

Abraham was a special servant of God. God told him, "Take everything you own, and go to the land I will show you." Abraham did as God told him. He packed his camels and left with his wife, Sarah.

They traveled through the desert and stopped to camp. God said, "Abraham, look up at the sky! Can you count the stars? That's how many children I will give you."

# COUNT THE ANIMALS

How many of each animal can you find in the picture?

dog

camel

donkey

# DOT-TO-DOT

Connect the dots to see what God is showing to Abraham.

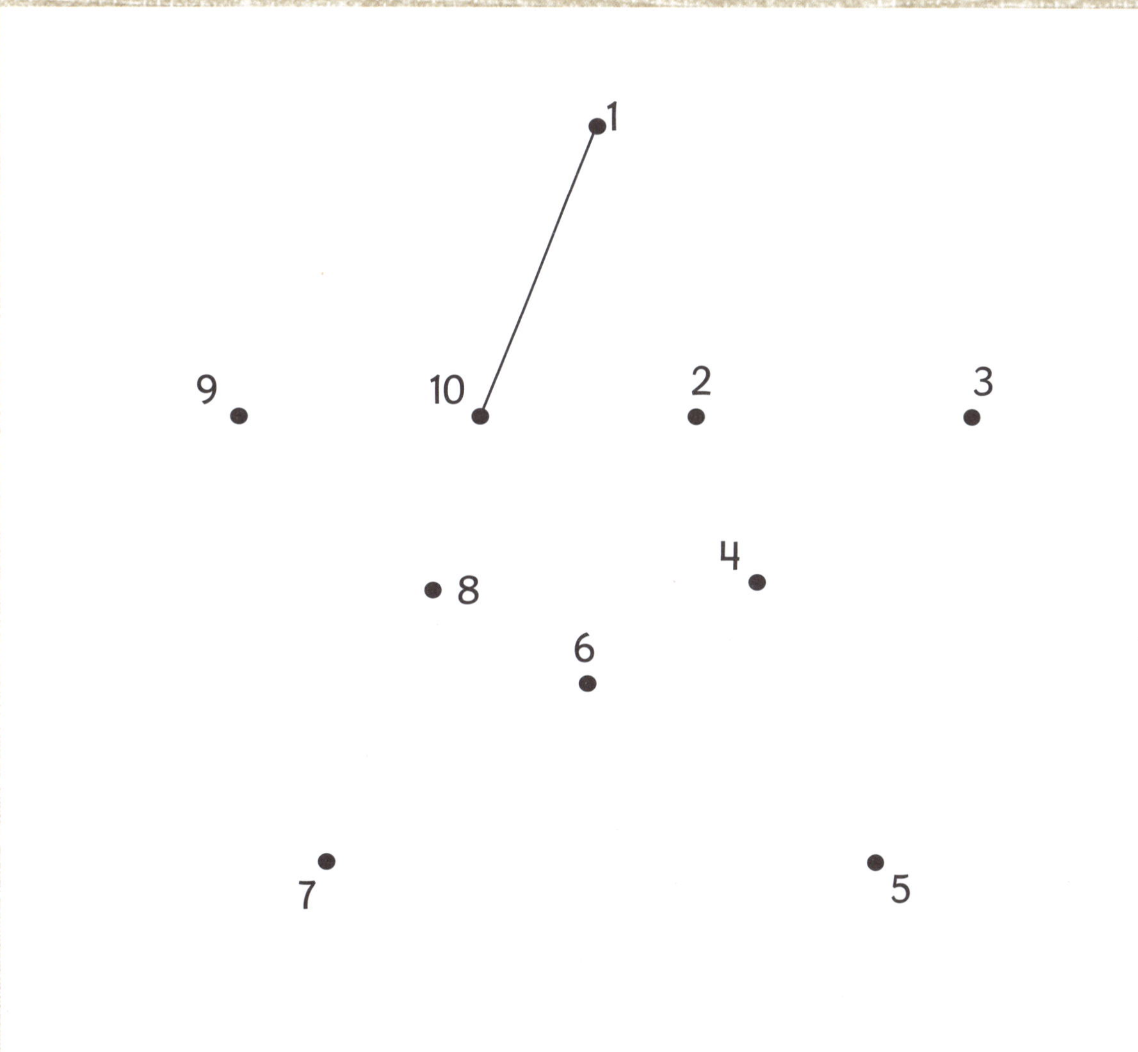

# Abraham's Great Big Family

Genesis 15:1–19; 18:1–19; 21:1–7

When Abraham and Sarah started getting old, they still had no children. But through all their journeys, they believed that God would give them the big family He had promised.

One day, three travelers came to Abraham's camp. One of them was God. He promised Abraham a son. But Sarah laughed and thought, "I'm too old to have a baby." The visitor said, "Why did Sarah laugh? Nothing is impossible for God." A year later, Sarah had a baby boy. They named him Isaac. Sarah was very happy and praised God for His wonderful gift.

Abraham and Sarah's family was very blessed because they followed God wherever He led them, even when God surprised them.

# SPOT THE DIFFERENCES

Can you find the 7 differences between these 2 pictures?

# COLOR ABRAHAM AND ISAAC

# Joseph and the Colorful Coat

Genesis 37

Isaac had a son named Jacob, and Jacob had twelve sons.

Jacob's favorite son was Joseph, and so Jacob gave Joseph an extra special coat. When Joseph's brothers saw that their father loved Joseph more than he loved them, they became jealous.

One night, Joseph dreamed that he was ruler. When he told his brothers about the dream, they laughed. "Do you really think you will rule over us?" Now they hated Joseph more than ever.

The brothers made a plan to get rid of Joseph. They took his beautiful coat and they threw him into an empty well.

When a caravan passed, they decided to sell him to the traders. Joseph was sold, and the caravan took him away to Egypt.

# GO TO EGYPT

Which road leads the caravan to Egypt?

# WORD SEARCH

Find the words hidden in the grid.

EGYPT

WELL

| F | C | I | W | K | N |
|---|---|---|---|---|---|
| J | O | S | E | P | H |
| A | A | Q | L | U | V |
| C | T | X | L | O | Y |
| O | D | R | E | A | M |
| B | E | G | Y | P | T |

JACOB

JOSEPH

COAT

DREAM

# Joseph Forgives His Brothers

Genesis 39:1–47:12

Joseph became a slave in Egypt. But God was with him. Joseph worked very hard. His master liked him very much, but his master's wife told a lie that caused Joseph to be thrown in jail! But even in jail, God was with Joseph and helped him.

Two years later, Pharaoh, the king of Egypt, had a dream. Joseph told Pharaoh that the dream meant there was going to be a famine. Pharaoh was so thankful that he let Joseph out of jail and put him in charge of storing food.

The famine finally came. Back in Canaan, Joseph's brothers were hungry. They went to Egypt to buy food. When they came to ask for food, they didn't even recognize Joseph, but he recognized them at once.

Finally Joseph said, "I am your brother! Don't be angry with yourselves for selling me as a slave. It was part of God's plan so that our family would not starve when the famine came!"

His brothers were overjoyed! Joseph had forgiven them for the cruel things they had done to him. Joseph's family moved to Egypt, and they all lived happily together.

# SPOT THE DIFFERENCES

Can you find the 7 differences between these 2 pictures?

# FIND THE PAIR

Find the 2 pictures of Joseph that are exactly the same.

# Baby Moses

Exodus 2:1–10

Long after Joseph died, a bad Pharaoh ruled Egypt. He didn't like that there were so many Hebrews in Egypt, so he forced them to become slaves. Then he ordered his soldiers to kill the Hebrew babies.

One Hebrew woman put her baby in a basket and sent him floating down the river. She hoped God would save him.

The princess of Egypt went down to the river. When she saw the basket, she took the baby out of the river and named him Moses.

Moses became the son of the princess. Moses grew up in Pharaoh's palace just like a real prince.

# FIND THE BASKET

Help the princess find baby Moses.

# FIND THE RIGHT SHADOW

Draw a line to connect each picture to its shadow.

# Moses Hears the Call of God

Exodus 1:11–4:17

Even though Moses lived like a prince, he knew that he was a Hebrew. It made him sad to see how the Egyptians mistreated his people. One day, he saw an Egyptian hitting a Hebrew. When no one was looking, Moses killed the Egyptian. Pharaoh came after him, so Moses ran away.

Moses settled in a new land, but God had not forgotten His plan for Moses. While Moses was tending his sheep, God spoke to him from a burning bush! God's voice said, "Moses, I have chosen you to lead My people out of Egypt."

# FOLLOW THE LETTERS

Follow each letter and write it down in the square at the bottom. You will discover a word from the story.

# PUZZLE GAME

Find out where the missing pieces belong and draw a line to their correct places.

A

B

C

D

# Moses Leads God's People

Exodus 5–16

Moses obeyed God and went to the king of Egypt.

"Let my people go!" he said. But the king was very stubborn. He told Moses, "No, your people cannot go."

God punished the Egyptians for this. He sent ten plagues to destroy Egypt. First, He made their water go bad. Then He sent frogs, insects, sickness, and storms! When many Egyptians died, Pharaoh at last changed his mind. He told Moses, "Get out of here, and don't ever come back!"

The king chased Moses and the Hebrew people to the edge of the Red Sea. God told Moses to lift his hands, and the sea opened up! The people walked safely to the other side. When Pharaoh's army tried to follow them, God closed the waters.

Moses and all of God's people were safe.

God gave Moses the power to do miracles. He also led Moses to the edge of the promised land. "This land flows with milk and honey," God said. "And it belongs to My people."

# REACH THE RED SEA

Find the road that Moses and the Hebrew people took to reach the Red Sea.

# SPOT THE DIFFERENCES

Can you find 7 differences between these 2 pictures?

# General Joshua and the Promised Land

Joshua 1, 6

Joshua was Moses's helper. Joshua loved God with all his heart. When Moses died, God told Joshua, "Be brave. You will now lead My people to the promised land. And I will be with you wherever you go."

The first city Joshua went to was Jericho. The people there were trembling with fear and shut all the city gates. No one could go in or out. Yet God had a plan. He told Joshua, "March around the city of Jericho once every day. On the seventh day, shout praises and blow your horns. Jericho will be yours!" Joshua did just as God told him. The priests went first, carrying trumpets. Then came the army and the rest of the Israelites. One, two, three, four, five, six days! On the seventh day, they blasted their horns, and the ground began to shake.

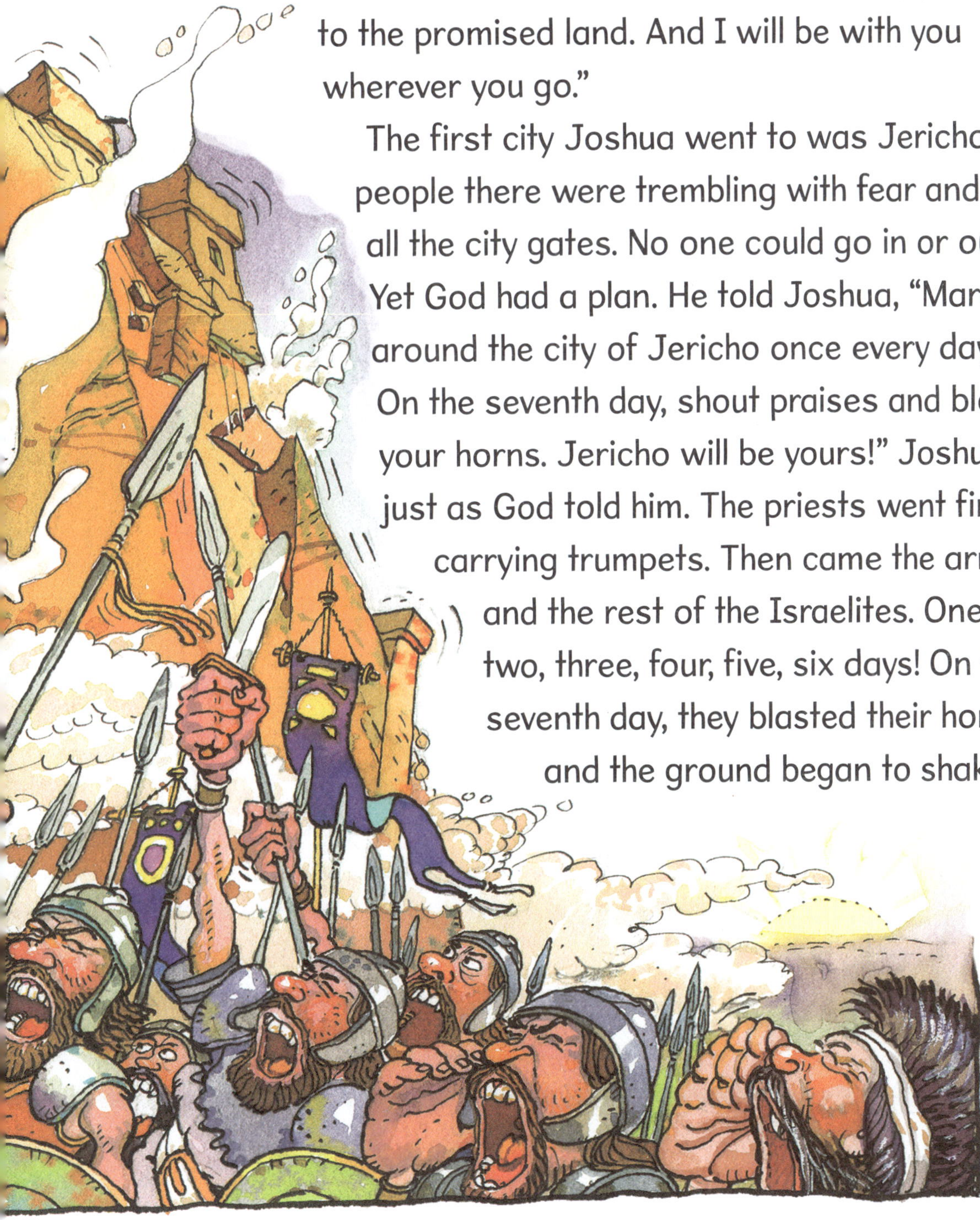

# COUNT THE OBJECTS

Count how many objects are in each box and write down the number in the circle.

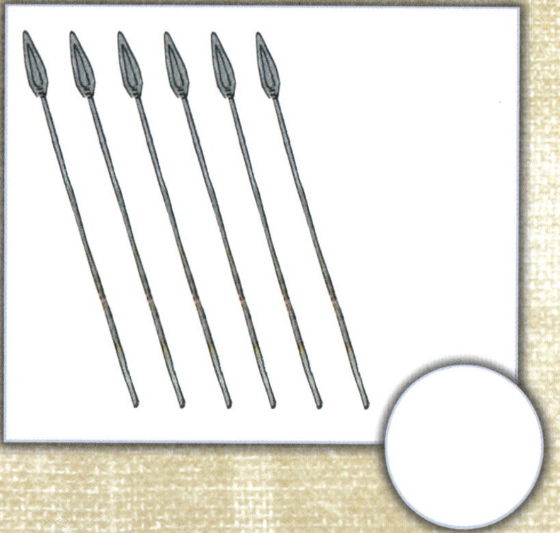

# ADD UP

Add up the objects and write down the number for each line.

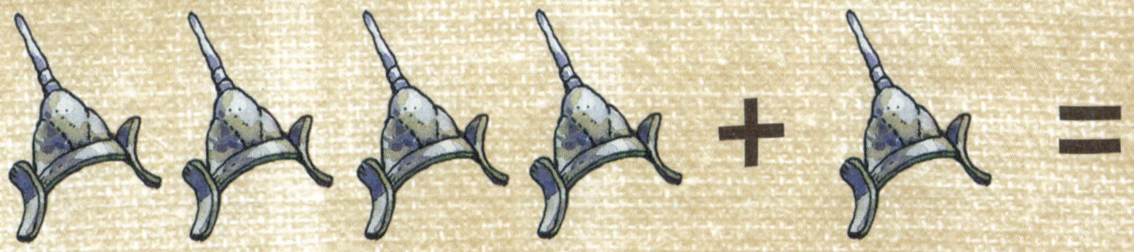

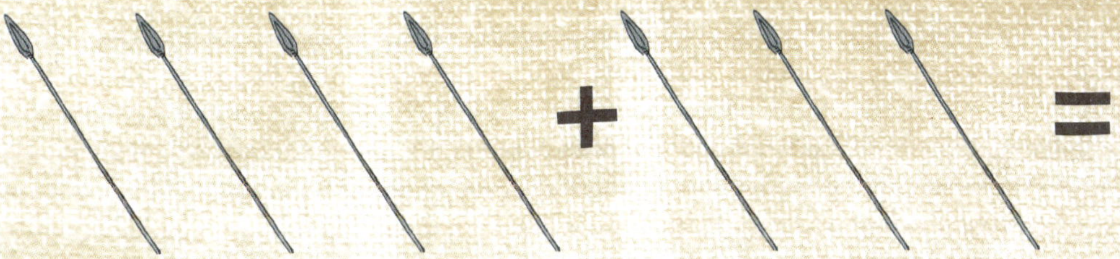

# Gideon and the Battle

Judges 6–7

The people of Israel were in trouble. The cruel Midianites ruled over their land and took their food and animals. They cried out to God for help.

One day, a young man named Gideon saw an angel sitting under a tree. "God wants you to save Israel," the angel said. "Me?" Gideon could not believe it. He wasn't sure that he would be able to beat the Midianites, but God promised to be with him.

The enemy was getting closer. Gideon rounded up a huge army. But God told Gideon he only needed a very small army of three hundred soldiers to fight the Midianites because God would be with them. Gideon gave each soldier a torch for one hand and a trumpet for the other.

Then they marched toward the Midianites. At the edge of the camp, the Israelites blew their horns. Then they gave a great shout. In the valley below, the Midianites became terrified and ran away.

God's people won the battle against their enemy!

# FIND THE RIGHT SHADOW

Draw a line to connect each picture to its shadow.

# WORD SEARCH

Find the words hidden in the grid.

ENEMY

CAMP

HORN

TORCH

CAMEL

| B | D | C | A | M | P |
|---|---|---|---|---|---|
| T | S | E | R | I | U |
| O | K | N | M | F | H |
| R | G | E | Y | V | O |
| C | A | M | E | L | R |
| H | X | Y | J | Q | N |

ARMY

# Samson the Mighty

Judges 13–16

When Samson was born, God blessed him and made him very strong. Someday, Samson was going to save his people from their enemies. As a sign of his special purpose, God told Samson's parents that they should never cut his hair.

Samson became stronger and stronger the longer his hair grew.

When his enemies came to arrest him, they tied him with rope. Then suddenly, Samson broke the ropes off!

# DOT-TO-DOT

One day, an animal attacked Samson, but Samson was very strong and threw him off. Connect the dots to see what animal it was.

# COLOR SAMSON

# God Rewards Ruth's Loyalty

Ruth 1–4

There was a woman from Israel named Naomi. She had two sons. One of them was married to a woman named Ruth, who was from a place called Moab.

Naomi's husband died, and her sons died too. So Naomi told Ruth to go home. But Ruth said, "I won't leave you. Where you go I will go. Your people will be my people, and your God will be my God."

Ruth and Naomi traveled to Bethlehem. It was a long journey. Naomi and Ruth needed food, so Ruth went to the fields and picked

up the leftover grain from a field belonging to a man named Boaz.

Naomi hoped Boaz would help Ruth find a new husband.

Soon, Boaz and Ruth were married!

# FIND RUTH'S HUSBAND

Help Ruth find Boaz.

# HIDDEN WHEAT GRASSES

Find 7 hidden wheat grasses in the picture.

# God Chooses David

1 Samuel 16:1–13

One day, God told His prophet Samuel to go to the home of a man named Jesse. One of Jesse's sons was going to be the new king.

Samuel looked at each of Jesse's big, strong sons. "Do you have any other sons?" Samuel asked.

"Only David, the smallest," Jesse answered, "but he is taking care of the sheep."

Samuel had him brought in. When Samuel saw David, God told him

that this was the one to be king. Samuel poured oil on David's head. From that day on, David was powerful in all he did.

# FIND THE PAIR

Find the 2 pictures of David and Samuel that are exactly the same.

# COLOR BY NUMBERS

Color the picture below using the color code, and you will see what Samuel used to show that David was the chosen king.

1 Yellow   2 Blue   3 Orange   4 Brown

# David Fights Goliath

1 Samuel 17

At this time, the Philistines were attacking Israel. They had a hero named Goliath. He was a giant. Goliath said, "Send someone to fight me!" David's brothers and the other soldiers were too afraid. But David said, "I will fight Goliath!" He collected five smooth stones and put them in his bag. Then David went right up to Goliath.

"You come with a sword, but I come in the name of the Lord!" David shouted. He pulled out a stone and swung his slingshot. The stone hit Goliath right in the forehead!

The giant fell facedown onto the ground, and all the other Philistines ran away. David was a hero! He became the next king of Israel.

# DOT-TO-DOT

Connect the dots to see what Goliath was holding to fight David.

# FIND THE STONES

Help David find the stones to fight Goliath.

# The Wisdom of King Solomon

1 Kings 3:1–28; 4:29–34

After King David died, his son Solomon ruled Israel. God came to him in a dream. Solomon said, "Lord, make me wise so that I will know right from wrong."

God made Solomon the wisest king who ever lived.

One time two women came to him. They were fighting over a baby. "He's my son!" shouted one woman. "No! He's mine!" said the other. It seemed impossible to know who the real mother was, but wise Solomon had a plan to find out.

"Cut the baby in half," he said. The mother of the child cried, "Give her the baby, but don't hurt him!" Now Solomon knew who had told the truth.

The people of Israel heard the story, and realized how wise Solomon was.

God gave Solomon a special gift to understand many things.

# SPOT THE DIFFERENCES

Find the 7 differences between these 2 pictures.

# FIND THE PAIR

Find the 2 pictures that are exactly the same.

# Elijah the Prophet

1 Kings 17

Elijah was God's special prophet. God told Elijah, "I am going to send a drought. No rain will fall for a long time."

God promised to take care of Elijah. He told Elijah to hide out in the wilderness. God sent ravens with food for Elijah to eat.

After a while, God spoke to Elijah again and told him to go to see a poor woman and her son. Elijah asked her for bread, but she had only a tiny bit of flour and oil. Elijah promised that if she fed him, she and her son would have plenty to eat. She made food for Elijah, and then God rewarded her. Her flour and oil never ran out!

While Elijah hid in the wilderness, who brought him bread and meat to eat every morning and every evening during the drought? He drank water from a brook until it dried up because there was no more rain.

# FIND THE POOR WOMAN

Help Elijah find the road to go to see the poor woman.

# FIND THE DIFFERENT ONE

On each line, find the picture that is different.

# Queen Esther Saves Her People

Esther 2–8

The king was looking for a wife. He gathered the most beautiful women from all around. Esther was one of them. Everyone liked

Esther because she was so beautiful and good. When the king met her, he chose her as his wife. The king didn't know she was a Jew.

Esther's cousin came to visit her. He would not bow to anybody except God. This made Haman, one of the king's officials, furious. "We must kill the Jews!" Haman told the king. So the king sent out an order for all the Jews to be put to death.

Esther felt sad and worried about her people. She decided God would want her to try to talk to the king, even if the king got angry with her. "Please save the Jews," she pleaded. "They are my people!"

The king listened to Esther and changed his order.

# ONE SINGLE ONE

Cross out all the objects that you find more than once in the grid, and circle the last one that is left.

# COLOR ESTHER

# Daniel and the Lions

Jeremiah 52; Daniel 1, 6

There was a terrible war in Israel. The king of Babylon attacked Jerusalem and took away many Israelites to his own land.

One of the prisoners was a boy named Daniel. Daniel was the king's favorite servant. He was wise and loyal and the king made him an important leader. The other leaders were jealous. They wanted to get rid of Daniel. So they planned a trick. They got the king to order everyone to pray only to the king himself. But Daniel would only pray to God. "Throw him in the lions' den!" his enemies said.

Though the king loved Daniel, he felt forced to punish him. So Daniel was thrown into a den of lions. In the darkness, Daniel prayed to the Lord. God sent angels to shut the lions' mouths. The next morning, the king rushed to the den to see what had happened. Daniel was safe.

# FIND THE RIGHT SHADOW

Which shadow belongs to Daniel? Circle it.

# COUNT THE ANIMALS

Count how many of the following animals you find in the picture, and write the number in the boxes.

☐ lion

☐ bat

☐ mouse

# Jonah and the Big Fish

Jonah 1–3

In a town called Nineveh, the people were doing bad things. God chose Jonah to go tell them to stop sinning. Jonah didn't want to go because the people there were his enemies. Instead, he thought he could run away by getting on a boat that was going in the opposite direction.

God sent a storm. The sailors trembled. Jonah told them, "It's my fault. I thought I could run away from God. Throw me overboard!" The sailors threw Jonah over, and the storm stopped. God sent a giant fish to swallow Jonah up! Jonah prayed from inside the fish.

He told God how sorry he was for trying to run away. Jonah had learned his lesson. So God told the fish to spit Jonah onto a beach. God said again, “Go to Nineveh!” This time Jonah obeyed. He told the people to turn their hearts to God, and they listened.

# FIND THE ODD ONE

Find which fish or seashell is not in the picture with Jonah.

# MATCH THE PAIRS

Draw a line to connect the 2 parts of the same animal.

THE NEW
TESTAMENT

# Mary and Joseph

Luke 1:26–38; 2:1–7

Mary was a young girl who lived in Nazareth. She had a pure heart, and she loved God. Mary was engaged to a carpenter named Joseph. God sent an angel to Mary. "I am Gabriel," the angel said. "I've come with good news! You will give birth to God's only Son." Mary answered the angel, "I am the Lord's servant. May His will be done."

The king gave an order that everyone had to go to their hometown to be counted. So Joseph and Mary went on a long journey to Bethlehem, where Joseph was from. Mary rode on the back of a donkey.

# PUZZLE GAME

Find out where the missing pieces belong and draw a line to their correct places.

# COLOR MARY AND JOSEPH

## The First Christmas

Luke 2

It was time for Jesus to be born! Mary wrapped Him lovingly in cloths and laid him in a manger, the animals' feeding box.

The angels in heaven rejoiced. God's Son had arrived!

Nearby, shepherds were watching their sheep. An angel appeared to them, saying, "I bring you good news—Christ is born!" The shepherds hurried to see Jesus, and then went and told other people about Him.

# WORD SEARCH

Find the words hidden in the grid.

| | | | | | |
|---|---|---|---|---|---|
| J | E | S | U | S | P |
| C | D | A | I | H | T |
| O | M | Q | X | E | B |
| W | A | N | G | E | L |
| F | R | U | A | P | K |
| V | Y | B | A | B | Y |

ANGEL

COW

MARY

BABY

JESUS

SHEEP

# COUNT THE ANIMALS

Count how many animals are in each box and write down the number in the circle.

## The Wise Men

Matthew 2:1–12

In a faraway country, some wise men also learned about Jesus. God put a special star in the sky to lead them to where Jesus was.

After many months, they arrived. They were so happy!

They brought expensive gifts of gold, frankincense, and myrrh. They knew Jesus was the "king of the Jews," and they bowed down and worshipped Him.

# SPOT THE DIFFERENCES

Can you find the 7 differences between these 2 pictures?

# LOOK FOR BABY JESUS

Draw over the line that goes from the wise men to baby Jesus.

# Jesus Chooses His Disciples

Matthew 4:18–22; Luke 5:1–11

Jesus grew up.

One day, he saw two brothers named Simon and Andrew throwing their nets into the sea.

Jesus told the fishermen, “Let down your nets.” They obeyed. When they pulled the nets in again, they were full of fish! The fishermen were amazed.

Jesus said to them, “Follow Me. I will make you fishers of people instead.” Simon and Andrew left their nets and followed Jesus.

As they walked along the sea, Jesus called to two men named James and John who were in a boat. They also followed Jesus.

Jesus chose twelve men in all.

"Follow Me," Jesus said to the men.

# FIND THE DIFFERENT ONE

Find the picture of Jesus and Simon that is different from the others.

1

2

3

4

# PUZZLE GAME

Find out where the missing pieces belong and draw a line to their correct places.

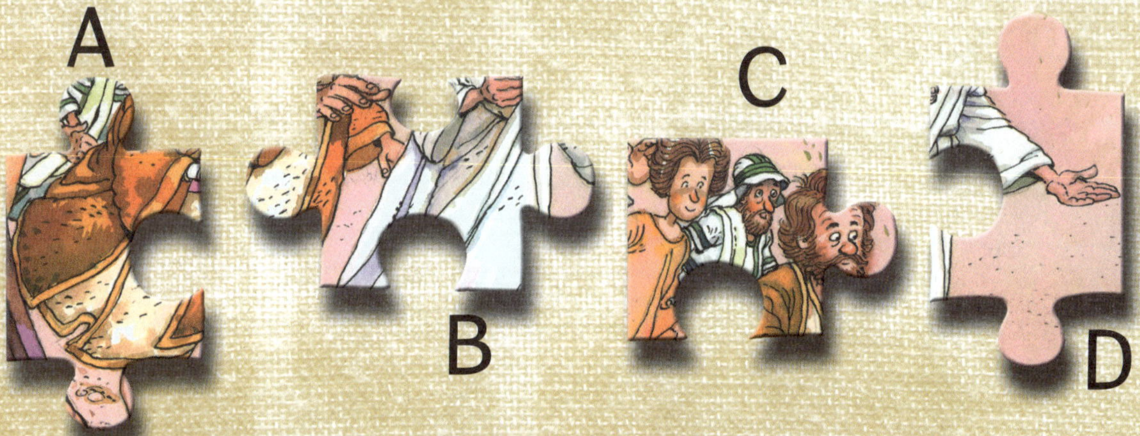

# The Stories of Jesus

Matthew 5–7

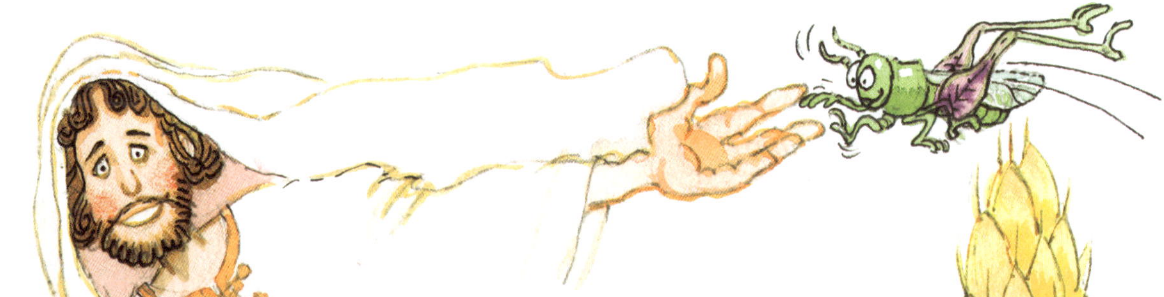

Jesus told many stories to teach people about God and His kingdom. Jesus said, "Blessed are those who suffer, because they will be rewarded in heaven." He taught that we should be kind to everyone, including our enemies, because God loves them. Jesus said to forgive people when they hurt us. In everything, we are to treat others the way we want to be treated. We are wise if we do what Jesus teaches.

If we plant goodness in our hearts, good things will grow from us.

# SMALLEST AND BIGGEST

Find the smallest and the biggest grasshopper.

# COUNT THE ANIMALS

Count how many animals are in each box and write down the number in the circle.

# The Loving Father

Luke 15:11–32

Jesus told this story: Once there was a man who had two sons. One day, the younger son told his father he wanted to leave home. He asked his father to give him a lot of money.

The son traveled to a land far away. There he spent all his father's money with bad friends. Then he was left all alone with no money to buy food. So he got a job taking care of pigs. He was so hungry, he wished he could eat the pigs' food.

Finally, he decided to go back to his father and ask for forgiveness. The father was watching for him and was so happy his son came home that they had a party.

# GO BACK HOME

Which road did the son take to go back to his father to ask for forgiveness? Find the right way.

# WORD SEARCH

Find the words hidden in the grid.

| Z | H | A | Q | H | F |
|---|---|---|---|---|---|
| B | E | J | C | U | A |
| S | F | B | A | G | T |
| M | O | N | E | Y | H |
| R | H | O | R | S | E |
| T | D | S | O | N | R |

MONEY

FATHER

SON

HUG

BAG

HORSE

# The Miracles of Jesus

John 2:1–11

Jesus went to a wedding in Galilee with His disciples. His mother, Mary, was also there. Later on in the evening, the wine ran out. The family hosting the wedding was embarrassed that they didn't have enough for their guests. So Mary asked Jesus to help.

All the jars were empty, so Jesus told the servants to fill them with water. Then Jesus turned the water into wine! The disciples smiled at one another. They knew that Jesus had done a miracle.

Jesus performed many, many miracles during his ministry on earth. But this miracle of turning water into wine was Jesus's first.

# ONE SINGLE ONE

Cross out all the objects that you find more than once in the grid, and circle the last one left.

# FIND OBJECTS

Find the following objects in the picture.

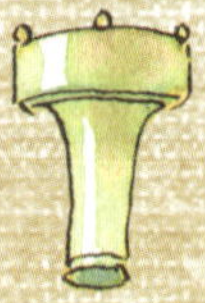

# Jesus Heals People

Matthew 8–9; Mark 2:1–12

People with all kinds of sicknesses came to Jesus, and He healed them. Some people had just gotten sick, and some people had been sick their whole lives.

One day, Jesus was teaching in a house. There was a crippled man outside who wanted to see Jesus, but the house was full. So the man's friends cut a hole in the roof and lowered him down.

Jesus saw that the man and his friends had faith. He said to the crippled man, "Get up!" The man obeyed. He could walk!

Everyone was amazed and they praised God. They had never seen anything like Jesus's healing!

# SPOT THE DIFFERENCES

Can you find 7 differences between these 2 pictures?

# WHO IS NOT IN THE PICTURE?

Can you find who is not in the house with Jesus?

1 

2 

3 

4 

5 

# Jesus Calms the Storm

Mark 4:35–41

One day, Jesus and His disciples were crossing a lake. Jesus fell asleep. Suddenly, a storm started. The boat began to fill with water. The disciples woke Jesus up, crying, "We are going to drown!"

Jesus commanded the storm to stop. All was calm. Then He said to His disciples, "Where is your faith?" The disciples were amazed—the wind and waves obeyed Jesus!

# FIND THE RIGHT SHADOW

Find which shadow belongs to Jesus.

# COUNT THE FISH

Write down the number of each type of fish you find in the picture.

flying fish

seahorse

butterfly fish

# Jesus Feeds People

John 6:10–14

Jesus was teaching a huge crowd when it began to get late. The disciples were worried. Where could they find food for so many people? There was nothing for them to eat.

A boy gave Jesus two fish and five loaves of bread. Jesus blessed the food. Then He began to break it . . . and filled basket after basket!

Over five thousand people ate until they were full. There were even twelve baskets of leftovers.

# FIND THE ANIMALS

Can you find the animals in the picture?

# WRITE THE WORDS

Look at each picture and word, and copy the names under each picture.

**FISH**

_ _ _ _

**BREAD**

_ _ _ _ _

**BASKET**

_ _ _ _ _ _

## Jesus Brings Lazarus to Life

John 11:1–44

Lazarus and his sisters were good friends with Jesus. One day, Lazarus got very sick. Jesus was away, so the sisters sent word to Him. Jesus waited a few days before He came to their village of Bethany. When He arrived, Lazarus was already dead. His sisters were very sad. Jesus went to the tomb and prayed. Then He shouted, “Lazarus, come out!” And Lazarus did. He was alive again!

Jesus did all His miracles so that the people who saw them would believe that God sent Jesus and gave Him the power to save the world from sin.

# COLOR THE PICTURE

# FOLLOW THE LETTERS

Follow each letter and write it down in the square at the bottom. You will discover a word from the story.

## Jesus Walks on Water

Matthew 14:22–36

One day, Jesus sent His disciples ahead in a boat while He went to pray. Soon a storm started to blow, tossing the boat. The disciples looked up and saw Jesus walking on the water toward them! At first they thought He was a ghost.

"Don't worry," Jesus said. "It's Me."

But Peter wasn't sure. "If it's really You, then let me come out to You," he said.

"Come," Jesus replied. Peter stepped out of the boat. He was walking on water too! Then he realized how strong the wind was and became afraid. Peter began to sink and cried, "Save me!"

So Jesus reached out His hand to catch Peter. "Where is your faith?" Jesus asked. When they climbed into the boat, the storm stopped immediately. Then the disciples worshipped Jesus and knew for sure that He was the Son of God.

# DRAW A BOAT

The disciples got into a boat to start their journey on the sea. Draw a boat.

# WORD SEARCH

Find the words hidden in the grid.

| | | | | | |
|---|---|---|---|---|---|
| J | N | Q | S | P | A |
| E | W | A | T | E | R |
| S | A | I | O | T | Y |
| U | L | N | R | E | L |
| S | K | U | M | R | K |
| V | B | O | A | T | Y |

# Jesus and the Children

Mark 10:13–16

Many children wanted to see Jesus too. The disciples tried to send them away, but Jesus said, "Let the little children come to Me!" Then He blessed the children.

"You must each become like a child in order to enter the kingdom of God," Jesus told His disciples.

Jesus loved children very much. He said that they are special because they don't worry about being important in the ways that grown-ups do.

# COUNT PEOPLE

How many men do you see in the picture below?

How many women do you see in the picture below?

How many children do you see in the picture below?

# FIND THE CLOTHING

Connect the part of the clothing to the person it belongs to.

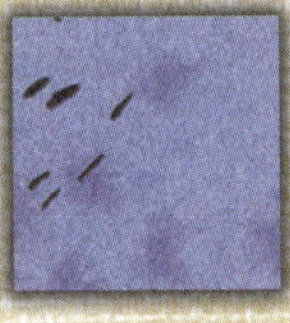

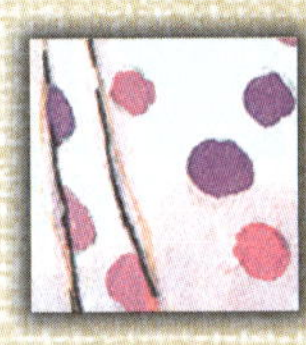

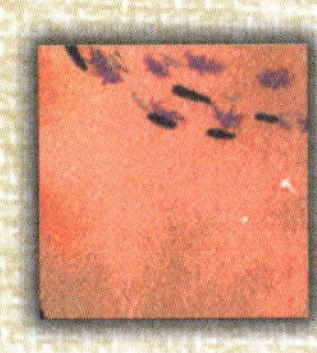

# Jesus in Jerusalem

Matthew 21:1–11

Jesus and His disciples came near Jerusalem. Jesus sent the disciples to find a donkey for Him. They put their coats on the donkey for Jesus to sit on.

Large crowds had gathered to welcome Him, spreading their coats and tree branches on the ground for Him to ride over.

Crowds in front of Him and behind Him all cried out, "Hosanna to the Son of David!"

"Blessed is He who comes in the name of the Lord! Hosanna!" the people shouted. They were so excited because they believed Jesus had come to save them.

# DRAW THE LEAF

Finish drawing the palm leaf.

# COUNT THE BRANCHES

How many branches can you find in the picture?

One of Jesus's disciples was about to betray Him.

# The Last Meal

Luke 22:7–23

It was time for the disciples to have their last supper with Jesus.

Jesus knew that He would soon return to His Father in heaven.

Jesus blessed the bread and wine and gave some to each disciple. He told them to remember Him when they ate from now on.

# FIND COLORS

Can you find these colors in the picture? Draw a line to connect the color in each box to the same color.

Blue

Pink

Purple

Red

Orange

# FIND THE CUPS

One cup is in Jesus's hand. Find 7 more matching cups in the picture.

# Jesus Is Arrested

Matthew 26:36–56

Jesus took His disciples to a garden. He was very sad and knelt on the ground. “Your will be done,” Jesus prayed to God.

Judas, one of Jesus’s disciples, brought the synagogue leaders and the soldiers to take Jesus away. “I must go,” Jesus said. “This is God’s plan.”

The disciples became afraid and ran away. Jesus's enemies took Him to be judged.

# FIND THE PAIR

Find the 2 pictures of Jesus and the soldier that are exactly the same.

# COPY THE WORD

Follow the dots to write the name of JESUS and then try to write it by yourself.

JESUS

---

# Peter Lies

Luke 22:54–62

When Jesus was taken away, Peter followed at a distance and waited outside the house where Jesus was. When the people saw Peter, they said to him, “You were with Jesus!”

“No I wasn’t,” Peter said. “I don’t even know Him.” Three times Peter lied about knowing Jesus. “I don’t know what you’re talking about!” he said.

Then a rooster crowed. Peter realized that he had betrayed Jesus, and he cried. He was very sorry for what he had done.

# SPOT THE DIFFERENCES

Find the 7 differences between these 2 pictures.

# COLOR THE ROOSTER

# Jesus on the Cross

Matthew 27:27–56; Luke 23:26–49

The soldiers hurt Jesus, then put Him on a wooden cross.

Over Jesus's head, the soldiers hung a sign that said, "This is Jesus, the King of the Jews." His enemies made fun of Him. "If You are really the Son of God, then do a miracle by getting down from the cross!" But Jesus knew that He needed to stay on the cross.

# DRAW A CROSS

Trace the dashes to make a cross. Color the cross.

# COUNT

How many of these animals and objects can you find in the picture?

sheep

spear

dog

horse

# Jesus Is Buried

Matthew 27:57–66; John 19:38–42

After Jesus died, His friends took His body off the cross. They wrapped Him in clean cloths, and then they laid Him in a tomb carved out of rock, like a cave. They rolled a big stone in front of the opening. Soldiers guarded the cave to make sure no one moved the rock.

Jesus's friends were very sad that He had died. They were going to miss Him very much.

Did you know that Jesus was willing to die on the cross? He was obeying His Father in heaven by dying to pay for the sins of all people.

# SPOT THE DIFFERENCES

Can you find the 7 differences between these 2 pictures?

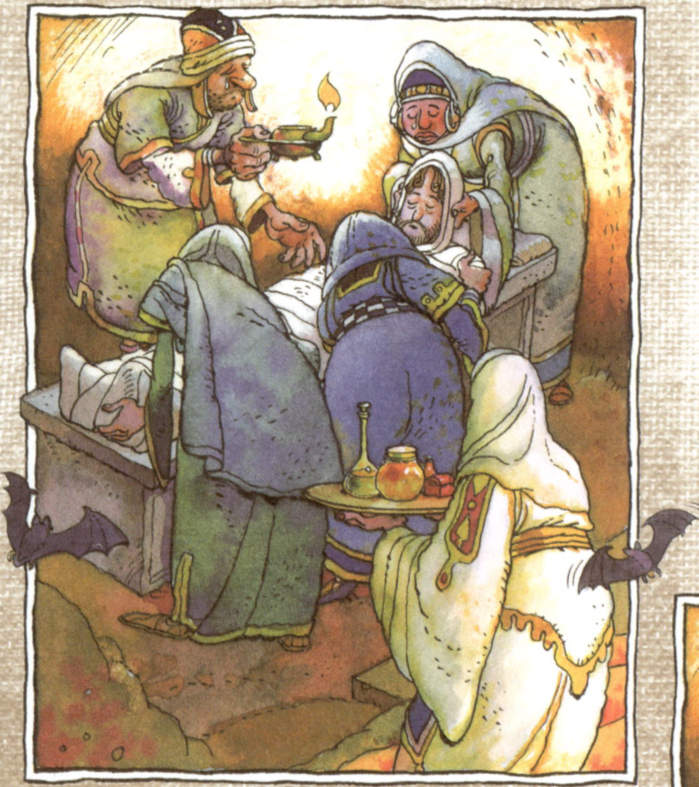

# COLOR BY NUMBERS

Color the picture below using the color code, and you will find what Jesus's friends used to see inside the cave.

1 Blue    2 Green    3 Yellow

# The First Easter

Matthew 28:1–10

After three days passed, some of Jesus's friends went to the tomb.

Suddenly, there was a great earthquake! An angel from heaven moved the stone away from the tomb's opening.

Then the angel spoke to the women. "Don't be afraid. I know you are looking for Jesus, but He isn't here. He is risen! Come and see for yourselves."

They went into the tomb. Jesus was gone!

"Go and tell His disciples that Jesus is risen from the dead," the angel said. "You will see Jesus again."

Jesus's friends were so happy to hear that He was alive again that they ran to tell His disciples.

# COUNT THE PEOPLE

How many women do you see in the picture?

How many soldiers can you find in the picture?

How many shoes do you see in the picture?

# FIND THE PAIR

Find the 2 pictures of the soldier that are exactly the same.

# Jesus Appears to the Disciples

John 20:19–23

One evening, the disciples were gathered together. They were hiding from people who wanted to hurt them for being friends with Jesus.

Suddenly, Jesus appeared! "Peace be with you," He said. The disciples were overjoyed to see Him. Jesus showed them His wounds. Then He gave them a special message—He was sending them into the world to do His work!

# HIDDEN BUTTERFLIES

Can you find the 5 butterflies in this picture?

# COLOR THE BUTTERFLY

# Jesus Goes to Heaven

Matthew 28:16–20; Acts 1:3–11

It was time for Jesus to return to heaven, so He led the disciples out of the city. There He told them, "Go and teach people everywhere that I came to pay for their sins."

Jesus gave the disciples the Holy Spirit. The Holy Spirit would help them do what God wanted them to do.

Then He was taken to heaven. The disciples were amazed. As He disappeared in a cloud, they worshipped God.

After Jesus went up to heaven, angels told the disciples that Jesus would come back again!

# FIND THE ODD HAT

Find which hat goes with each person. One doesn't belong to anyone!

# WHO IS LEFT?

Cross out all the people who appear twice in the grid. Who is left?

# Paul's Change of Heart

Acts 8:1–4; 9:1–18

After Jesus went to heaven, people who believed that He was God's Son were not treated well. One day, a man named Saul was on his way to Damascus to look for those Christians. He was going to bring them back to Jerusalem as prisoners. Suddenly, a light from heaven flashed around him!

Saul fell to the ground.

"Saul, why do you hurt Me?" he heard a voice say.

"Who are You?" Saul asked.

The voice answered, "I am Jesus. Now get up and go to the city."

Saul was still blind when he arrived in Damascus. A man named Ananias took him by the hand. "Jesus has sent me to give you back your sight," he said. All at once, Saul could see.

# GO TO DAMASCUS

Help Saul go to Damascus.

# COLOR SAUL ON HIS HORSE

# Paul Sings Praises

Acts 9:20–31; 16:16–40

Paul went to Jerusalem. He wanted to join the disciples, but they were afraid of him because of the bad things he had done before.

Finally, they learned how Paul had met Jesus and how he had preached in Damascus. So they all became friends, and together they taught others about Jesus. More and more people listened and believed.

Paul and his friends traveled far to spread the good news. One day, Paul and his friend Silas were thrown in jail. They prayed and sang praises to God. Suddenly, there was an earthquake and the prison doors opened! The guard was afraid and asked, "What must I do to be saved?" Paul and Silas answered that he must believe in Jesus. The guard and his whole family came to believe in God.

# SPOT THE DIFFERENCES

Find the 7 differences between these 2 pictures.

# COLOR BY NUMBERS

Color the picture below using the color code, and you will see what the guard used to release Paul and Silas.

1 Orange    2 Green

# Paul Spreads the Word

Acts 17–28

Paul traveled around the world and preached to people. "God loves you," he told them. "Believe in Jesus, and be one of God's children!"

The more Paul preached, the more his enemies tried to hurt him. Paul was very brave by answering everyone's questions. He was thrown in jail again and again, but he kept teaching people the truth about Jesus.

In jail, Paul wrote to churches and to friends and followers, telling them how to know God, how to live for Him, and how to love each other.

In one letter, Paul wrote, "Nothing can ever separate us from God's love."

# FIND THE RIGHT SHADOW

Connect the boats to their shadow.

# ADD UP THE BOATS

Add up the boats and write down the number for each line.

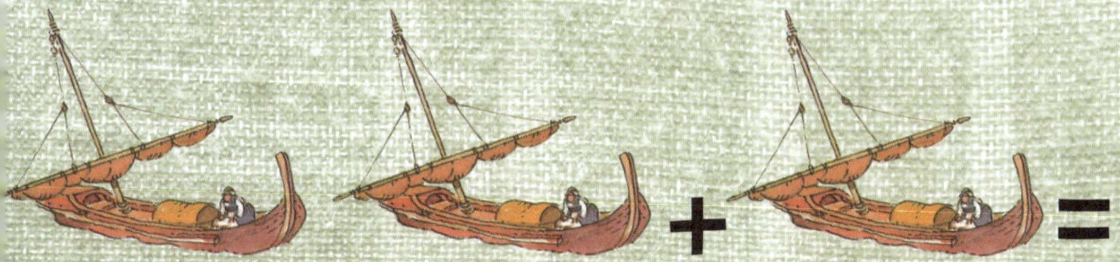

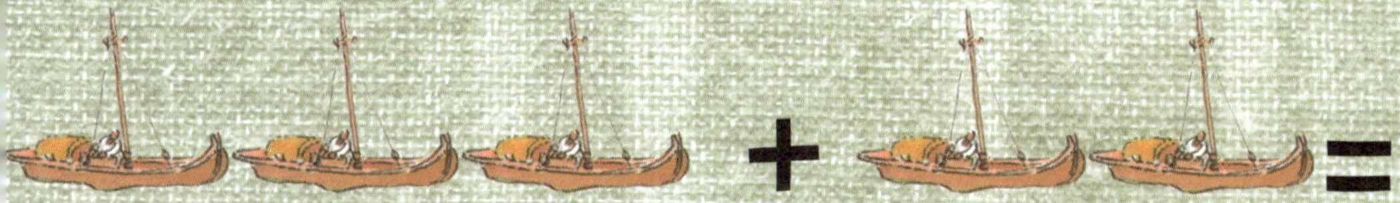

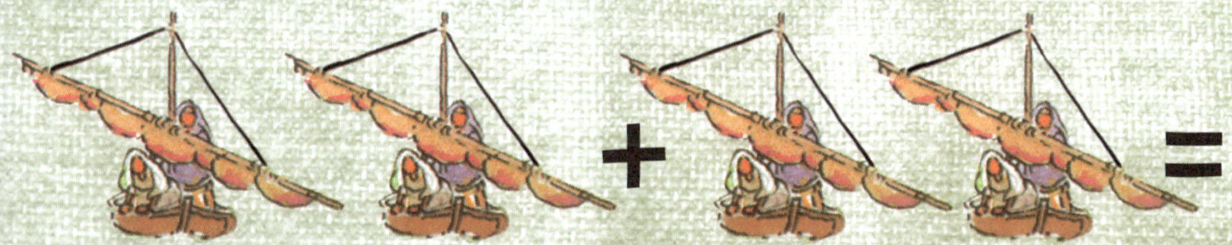

# God Promises a New World

1 John 2; Revelation 1, 21

John was one of Jesus's twelve disciples. He had watched Jesus perform miracles and listened closely to His teachings. When John was very old, he was given a special vision from God. God told him that Jesus was going to come back to earth soon. Then John saw heaven. Believers from every nation were singing praises around the throne of God. John saw a new heaven and a new earth. God and His people were no longer separated.

Jesus promises that we can live forever with Him.

# FIND THE DIFFERENT ONE

For each line, find which one is different.

1

2

3

4

1

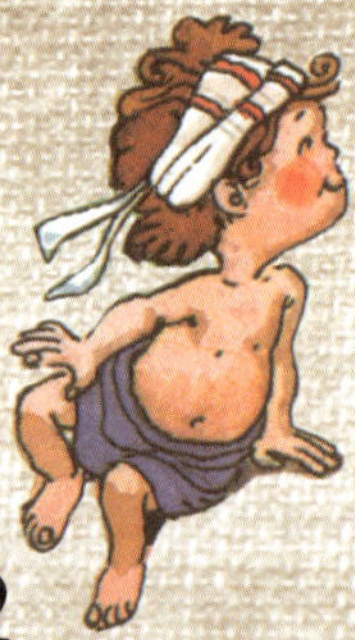
2

3

4

# COLOR BY NUMBERS

Color the picture below using the color code, and you will see what is watching Jesus and John as they talk.

1 Blue  2 Orange  3 Yellow

# Heaven

Revelation 21

Everyone who trusts in Jesus and lives for Him on earth will one day be in heaven with Jesus. In heaven there won't be any death, or pain, or even sad tears. There will only be joy and happiness in heaven.

Someday Jesus will return to earth, and He will make everything perfect. We will live in the joy of God's love forever.

God said, "I am making everything beautiful and new!"

# WORD SEARCH

Find the words hidden in the grid.

OWL

BEE

TURTLE

ANT

FROG

WORM

| | | | | | |
|---|---|---|---|---|---|
| B | F | A | N | T | A |
| D | R | A | T | U | W |
| J | O | W | L | R | O |
| M | G | N | R | T | R |
| O | K | U | M | L | M |
| U | R | B | E | E | Y |

# COLOR THE PICTURE

# GAME SOLUTIONS

## THE OLD TESTAMENT

**(pages 10–11) God Makes the World**
Picture 3 is different from the rest.

| A | E | X | I | L | S |
|---|---|---|---|---|---|
| D | A | R | K | T | U |
| P | R | M | O | O | N |
| S | T | A | R | G | W |
| Q | H | B | J | U | C |
| L | I | G | H | T | F |

**(pages 14–15) God Fills the Earth**
Add up: 2, 4 , 5, and 6 penguins

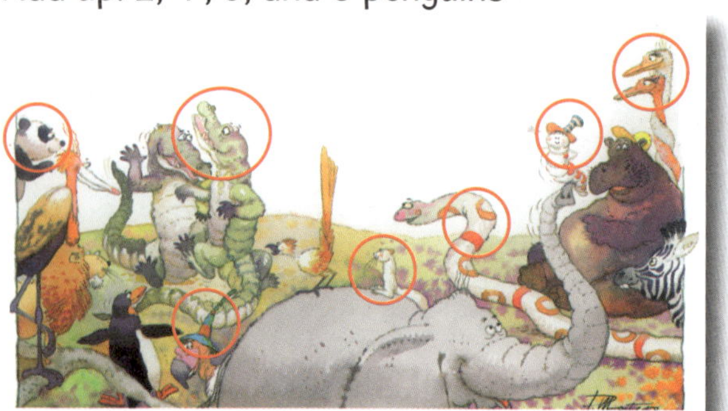

**(pages 18–19) Adam and Eve**

Dot-to-dot: an apple

**(pages 22–23) Cain and Abel**

## (pages 26–27) Noah and the Ark

## (pages 30–31) The Great Flood

Picture 2 is different from the rest.

## (pages 38–39) The Tower of Babel

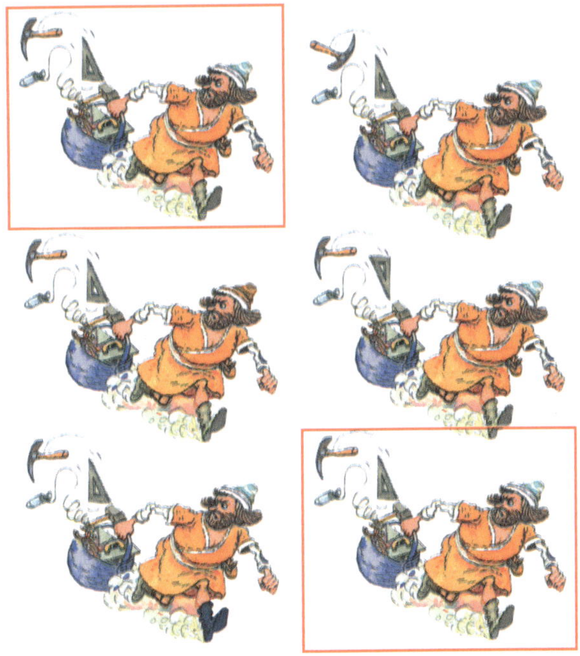

## (pages 42–43) Abraham Follows God

Count the animals: 1 dog; 2 donkeys; 5 camels

Dot-to-dot: a star

## (pages 46–47) Abraham's Great Big Family

## (pages 50–51) Joseph and the Colorful Coat

| F | C | I | W | K | N |
|---|---|---|---|---|---|
| J | O | S | E | P | H |
| A | A | Q | L | U | V |
| C | T | X | L | O | Y |
| O | D | R | E | A | M |
| B | E | G | Y | P | T |

## (pages 54–55) Joseph Forgives His Brothers

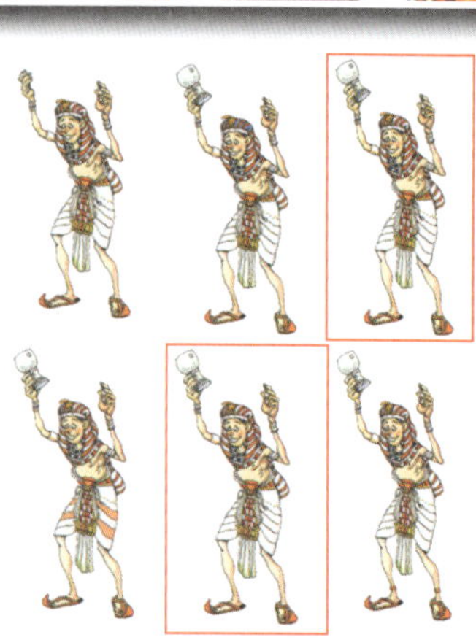

## (pages 58–59) Baby Moses

## (pages 62–63) Moses Hears the Call of God

Follow the letters: HEBREWS

**(pages 66–67) Moses Leads God's People**

**(pages 70–71) General Joshua and the Promised Land**

Count the objects: 5 helmets; 3 shields; 6 spears

Add up: 4 shields; 5 helmets; 7 spears

**(pages 74–75) Gideon and the Battle**

| B | D | C | A | M | P |
|---|---|---|---|---|---|
| T | S | E | R | I | U |
| O | K | N | M | F | H |
| R | G | E | Y | V | O |
| C | A | M | E | L | R |
| H | X | Y | J | Q | N |

**(pages 78–79) Samson the Mighty**

Dot-to-dot: a lion

**(pages 82–83) God Rewards Ruth's Loyalty**

**(pages 86–87) God Chooses David**

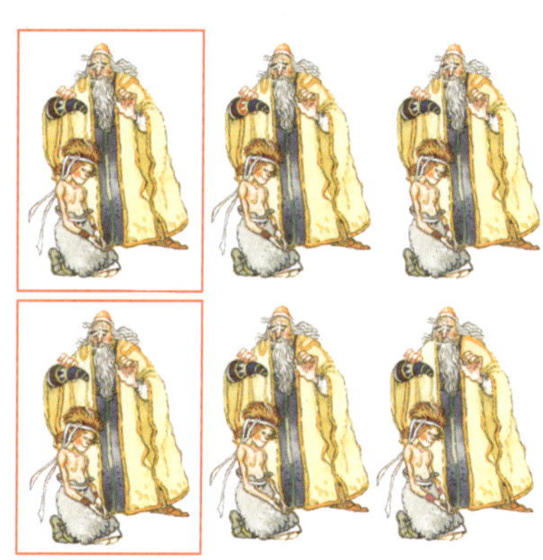

Color by numbers: an oil jar

**(pages 90–91) David Fights Goliath**
Dot-to-dot: a sword

**(pages 94–95) The Wisdom of King Solomon**

**(pages 98–99) Elijah the Prophet**

Picture 3 of Elijah is different from the rest.

Picture 4 of the raven is different from the rest.

Picture 2 of the lizard is different from the rest.

**(pages 102–103) Queen Esther Saves Her People**
The single one is:

**(pages 106–107) Daniel and the Lions**
Shadow 3 belongs to Daniel.
Count the animals: 6 lions; 3 mice; 1 bat

**(pages 110–111) Jonah and the Big Fish**
This fish is not in the picture with Jonah:

# THE NEW TESTAMENT

**(pages 116–117) Mary and Joseph**

**(pages 120–121) The First Christmas**

| | | | | | |
|---|---|---|---|---|---|
| J | E | S | U | S | P |
| C | D | A | I | H | T |
| O | M | Q | X | E | B |
| W | A | N | G | E | L |
| F | R | U | A | P | K |
| V | Y | B | A | B | Y |

Count the animals: 5 owls; 3 sheep; 2 cows

**(pages 124–125) The Wise Men**

**(pages 128–129) Jesus Chooses His Disciples**
Picture 3 is different from the rest.

**(pages 132–133) The Stories of Jesus**

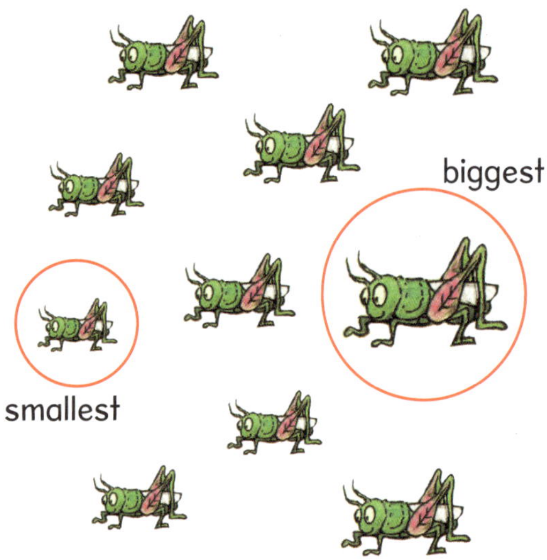


Count the animals: 2 mice; 4 field mice; 6 grasshoppers

**(pages 136–137) The Loving Father**

| Z | H | A | Q | H | F |
|---|---|---|---|---|---|
| B | E | J | C | U | A |
| S | F | B | A | G | T |
| M | O | N | E | Y | H |
| R | H | O | R | S | E |
| T | D | S | O | N | R |

**(pages 140–141) The Miracles of Jesus**

The single one is: 

**(pages 144–145) Jesus Heals People**

Who is not in the picture: 5

**(pages 148–149) Jesus Calms the Storm**

Shadow 2 belongs to Jesus.

Count the fish: 4 flying fish; 3 seahorses; 3 butterfly fish

**(pages 152–153) Jesus Feeds People**

**(pages 156–157) Jesus Brings Lazarus to Life**
Follow the letters: BETHANY

**(pages 160–161) Jesus Walks on Water**

| J | N | Q | S | P | A |
|---|---|---|---|---|---|
| E | W | A | T | E | R |
| S | A | I | O | T | Y |
| U | L | N | R | E | L |
| S | K | U | M | R | K |
| V | B | O | A | T | Y |

**(pages 164–165) Jesus and the Children**
Count people: 5 men; 3 women; 6 children

**(pages 168–169) Jesus in Jerusalem**
Count the branches: 12 branches

**(pages 172–173) The Last Meal**

**(pages 176–177) Jesus Is Arrested**

**(pages 180–181) Peter Lies**

**(pages 184–185) Jesus on the Cross**
Count: 5 sheep; 5 spears; 2 dogs; 3 horses

**(pages 188–189) Jesus Is Buried**

Color by numbers: an oil lamp

**(pages 192–193) The First Easter**
Count: 3 women; 2 soldiers; 9 shoes

**(pages 196–197) Jesus Appears to the Disciples**

**(pages 200–201) Jesus Goes to Heaven**
The odd hat is:

Who is left:

**(pages 204–205) Paul's Change of Heart**

### (pages 208–209) Paul Sings Praises

Color by numbers: a key

### (pages 212–213) Paul Spreads the Word

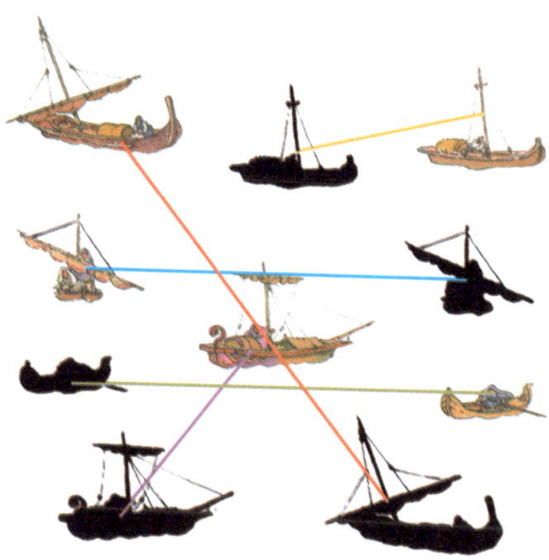

Add up the boats: 3, 5, 6, and 4 boats

### (pages 216–217) God Promises a New World

Picture 2 of John is different from the rest.

Picture 4 of the boy is different from the rest.

Color by numbers: a crab

### (pages 220–221) Heaven

| | | | | | |
|---|---|---|---|---|---|
| B | F | A | N | T | A |
| D | R | A | T | U | W |
| J | O | W | L | R | O |
| M | G | N | R | T | R |
| O | K | U | M | L | M |
| U | R | B | E | E | Y |

# Dear Parents,

Not only is this activity book fun and engaging, it is, above all, a journey through stories from the Bible that show how big and powerful God is, and how your child can live for Him in a world that doesn't make that easy.

Each Bible story is accompanied by creative, carefully crafted activities—finding key concepts in a word search, mazes and matchups, coloring important characters like Jesus and Mary and Moses, and more. When your child has finished this book, you can naturally move them to the next activity book (for ages 7 and up), which explores the same Bible stories in greater depth with more complex activities. Also perfect for an older brother or sister!

The activity books are designed to match up with *Big God, Little Me: An Ask and Learn Storybook Bible*. With 30 stories across 350 pages, it features the same rich, four-color artwork style in an easy-to-read format. As an extra bonus, the activity books include some lesser known stories not found in the Bible storybook.

We hope you'll love how this collection helps you encourage your child to know and love God

Sincerely,

The Kregel Team

978-0-8254-4595-8
hardcover

978-0-8254-4642-9
paperback

978-0-8254-4643-6
paperback